DEAD LOSSES
Useless Rulers from History

The Stories Live On

Some people think history is dead and buried. It all happened so long ago, it must be dead dull. Right? Wrong! The past never really goes away. Why? Because historical stories can live on *for ages*. It happens like this:

- Writers find out about the past from old pictures and old texts.

- They write stories about what they have found.

- You read the stories.

- The past comes back to life!

These stories can be dead interesting – and dead surprising too. They show us how life used to be – and even how people used to think. Just take a look over the page ...

Contents

If you want to learn the surprising truth about kings and queens from history, then you've come to the right place! The kings and queens in this book all have something else in common – they weren't much good at ruling. In fact many people have said they were dead losses. But why were they so unsuccessful?

Chapter 1
Could You Rule a Kingdom? 4
Find out about a ruler's steps to success.

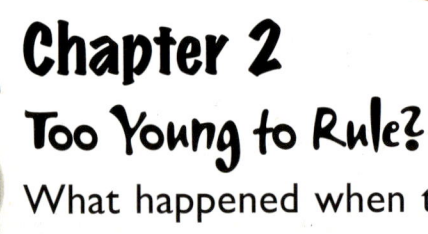

Chapter 2
Too Young to Rule? 9
What happened when the kids were left in charge?

Chapter 3
No Job for a Lady?   15
People used to say only a man could rule successfully. But were they right?

Chapter 4
Not Exactly There   19
Some rulers just didn't have their minds on the job at all. So what were they thinking about?

Chapter 5
A Job to Die For?   24
Find out how dead-loss rulers could lose more than just their jobs!

Timeline   30
Glossary and Index   32

Chapter 1
Could You Rule a Kingdom?

How hard can it be?

Being a **monarch** might sound like a fun job. But kings and queens in the past didn't just sit around all day. They had to do lots of things to be *seen* as successful.

I could be a successful queen. All I have to do is give orders!

I'd order pizza every night of the year!

Monarchs in history really had to **govern**. Today, in the UK, the **Prime Minister** and **Members of Parliament** do this. Monarchs in the past were far more hands-on. But what did they have to do?

Monarch Required

Excellent pay, all the food you can eat, luxurious living quarters, masses of servants, some foreign travel (usually to fight in wars).

You will need to:
- keep the kingdom safe from **invaders**
- make sure criminals are caught and punished
- be ready to listen to **subjects**' problems and help sort them out
- look super-strong, super-wise and generally superhuman
- be highly respected by all subjects.

Anyone applying should already be royal or come from an important and powerful family.

Keeping it in the Family

To be a monarch, it was incredibly important that you were in some way related to the ruler who had just died – or who you had just killed in battle! Ideally you were his son. You'll find out later why a daughter wasn't seen as quite so ideal.

> I was born to do this job!

> Hmm. You'd never have got it otherwise.

Going Down Well in History

Royal duties *did* change with the times but monarchs were always expected to work hard. That way, they would earn their subjects' respect and be seen as successful.

Many monarchs wanted to be remembered throughout history as successes too. So kings like Henry VIII, who ruled nearly 500 years ago, made sure they looked good in paintings that would live on after them.

"That's it, Mr Painter. Make me look handsome and powerful."

"I think *we'll* be the judge of that!"

But not everyone who sat on a throne was cut out to be a great ruler. In fact, quite a few English monarchs have gone down in history as real dead losses. It wasn't *always* their fault though. Some of them tried really hard to do the job. Yet for the reasons you'll find in this book, it just didn't work out.

"I think I'll have a snooze today."

"I'm afraid not, Sire. You've got a kingdom to rule."

Chapter 2
Too Young to Rule?

Can I rule now, please?

To be a successful ruler was hard. To be young and successful was even harder. A child didn't have the **authority** of an adult – and that meant trouble for everyone.

The Princes in the Tower

In the spring of 1483, life suddenly changed for young Prince Edward. He was just 12 years old when his father, King Edward IV, died. He was now supposed to be crowned King Edward V. But that wasn't how things turned out at all ...

Edward was far too young to do any real ruling. So his uncle Richard became 'Lord Protector'. This meant Richard did all the day-to-day ruling.

The king is dead! Long live the ... boy?

Meanwhile Edward was still supposed to be king. But Richard kept him and his younger brother hidden away in the Tower of London (which was a royal palace at the time).

They say it's a palace ... but it's more like a prison.

I've got a bad feeling about this.

Edward was never crowned king and then he and his brother mysteriously disappeared. In the autumn of 1483, Richard had *himself* crowned King Richard III and ruled for two years. We still don't know for sure what happened to young Edward and his brother, but there were rumours that King Richard had arranged to have the boys murdered.

In 1485, kings didn't give interviews because newspapers and television didn't exist. But if they had, imagine what King Richard might have said ...

Crown TV: Congratulations on your second anniversary as king, Sire.

Richard: Thank you! It's been great. Being a monarch is a job for a man not a boy! Thanks to my firm rule this kingdom is now in fine shape.

Crown TV: But, Sire, people are ... er ... wondering what has happened to young Edward and his brother.

Richard: Let's look to the present not the past! Everyone knows exactly who the boss is now. I make sure of that by touring the country and punishing wrong-doers.

Crown TV: True. But young Edward is meant to be king.

Richard: But we all know that a child cannot keep the peace. What's more, this country could be attacked at any time. Could a child lead troops against an army of invaders?

Crown TV: Even so, some people are saying you've had the boys ... um ... murdered!

continues over page →

Richard: Let us look forward! I shall carry on ruling for many more glorious years. No one will be talking then about missing princes.

Crown TV: Well, I'm not sure people will forget.

Richard: Let's all agree that child rulers have absolutely no authority. That's why Edward was never crowned king.

Crown TV: Er ... that's not really why he wasn't crowned.

Richard: We should never allow a child to sit on the throne of this wonderful country again. Now if you'll excuse me, I've just heard that I have some invaders to defeat.

Note: This interview happened just before the invaders arrived and killed King Richard. So at least we know how *he* died!

There's always fighting when the king is a child.

All the grown-ups think they can do a better job.

So were there any more child rulers after Edward V? Oh yes!

It's Happening All Over Again!

Just over 50 years later, another little lad came to the throne. This king – Edward VI – was actually crowned, but at nine years of age he was even younger than Edward V. Could he now succeed as a ruler, or would the grown-ups mess things up again?

"But he's just a little boy!"

"How can a kid boss grown-ups about, even if he is a king?"

Almost as soon as Edward was crowned king, his uncle stepped in and made himself Lord Protector. But not long after, a **courtier**, John Dudley, pushed *him* aside to take charge. The people thought both men were selfish and untrustworthy. Then after six unhappy years, poor young Edward VI fell ill and died.

You're really not our proper king.

You can't tell us to do a thing!

Both young Edwards were dead losses as kings because they never actually got to rule. People needed an adult monarch to respect and obey. But did that mean things would be fine for *any* adult who ruled? Not always, as you'll soon see.

Chapter 3
No Job for a Lady?

That's what you think!

The monarch after young Edward VI was 37 years old. So, definitely a grown-up. This monarch was also related to the last ruler. Sounds good so far. But many people were sure this new person would be a dead-loss ruler too. Why? Because she was a woman! Believe it or not, people used to think ruling was a man's job!

Seriously, how can a queen lead an army?

Women should obey men.

Yes, men have authority, women don't.

For 500 years, England had been ruled by 23 kings in a row. Then in 1553, Mary I became the first ruling queen. Soon Mary's husband, Philip II of Spain, dragged England into a war between the Spanish and the French. That didn't seem acceptable to the English at all.

If newspapers had existed, imagine what they might have said ...

The Tudor Times

It's Not Our Fight!

The new war with France is proving most unpopular. The people are up in arms. "It will not do," said one angry farmer. "France and Spain have fallen out. What's that got to do with us?"

The people of this great country want to know why their **taxes** are paying for this war. The queen refused to comment. Let's hope this war ends soon — and that we win!

The war did not go well for England and made some people like Mary even less.

But Mary's problems did not stop there. Monarchs used to have the right to tell their subjects how to worship. But some English Christians wanted to worship in new ways. Mary wasn't happy with this. She preferred the old ways. So she made an example of 300 people who would not obey her. How? By having them burned to death.

After ruling for just five unsuccessful years, Mary died. She didn't have any children to take over from her, so the next in line to the throne was her younger sister, Elizabeth. How would the *second* ruling queen in 500 years turn out?

A New Role Model

Queen Elizabeth I didn't find ruling easy either, but she gave the job her complete attention. She kept good order in the country, and wasn't as bossy as her sister when it came to how her subjects worshipped. She also avoided husband trouble by not getting married!

As a result, Elizabeth ruled England not for five years like Mary, but for nearly 50 years. After that, it was hard to say that ruling wasn't a job for a lady!

> I'd follow her into battle!

> I'd follow her anywhere!

> She's better than a king!

> Long live the queen!

Mary I really wasn't England's coolest ruler. But Elizabeth killed off the idea that *all* ruling queens were a dead loss. Few monarchs worked as hard as she did. In fact, some didn't have their minds on the job at all ...

Chapter 4
Not Exactly There

Sorry, what?

There was one sure way for a monarch to be seen as a dead loss: by failing to **devote** himself (or herself) to the job. Here are four monarchs who *didn't* put ruling first. In fact, at times they hardly seemed to be there at all.

Wish You Were Here

King Richard I ruled England from 1189 to 1199.

Amount of time the English people saw him: just six months.

Reason for absence: living abroad, fighting wars of little use to England.

Who paid his expenses? England's people, through their taxes.

How did he die? From a wound he got in one of his wars abroad.

Was he a good ruler for England? No, a bit of a dead loss.

Dear English people,

Having a great war. Wish you were here. Could use a little extra cash from you for swords and stuff.

Thanks, King Richard

English people
England

Strangely, we now remember this King Richard as 'Richard the Lionheart' – because he was such a brave warrior.

> Richard the Lionheart? Richard the Long-distance Ruler, more like.

Praying for England

Our second absent monarch, King Henry VI, wasn't a warrior like Richard I. Nor did he spend much time abroad. He was king from 1422 until 1461, yet he hardly did any proper ruling at all. Why? Because he spent so much time praying and reading the Bible. Meanwhile, his kingdom was falling apart.

All over England, with the king not around to keep the peace, fights broke out. Two men were actually put on trial for calling their king a dead loss! They said he did so little, it was like having no king at all.

Do you think he'll still be king next year?

He hasn't got a prayer.

In 1461, King Henry VI was knocked off his throne – by a courtier, Edward of York, who really *did* want to rule.

The Vanishing Queen

In 1861, 400 years after King Henry VI, a third monarch disappeared. Queen Victoria was on the throne. By now, most of the actual governing was done by **Parliament**. But people still liked to see their king or queen. After all, they helped pay the monarch's expenses through their taxes! So how did Queen Victoria 'go missing'?

When Victoria's husband, Albert, died, the queen was heartbroken. She dressed in black and shut herself away – for nearly 40 years! Many of her subjects were not impressed.

> Her husband has been dead for years.

> closed

> Will she *ever* get over the loss?

Unlike Henry VI, Victoria had Parliament to run the country for her, so she was allowed to stick around. She celebrated first 50, then 60 years on the throne. By the time she died in 1901, Victoria had become more respected. For although she hadn't done much ruling, her kingdom was still in quite good shape.

Because her Parliament were so good, Victoria hasn't gone down in history as a dead loss. But the same cannot be said about her great-grandson, our fourth and last monarch who *really* wasn't devoted to his job as king.

A Job for Life?

In 1936, Edward VIII came to the throne. He had been a popular prince, so surely he would be a popular king? But he set his heart on marrying a lady called Mrs Wallis Simpson. Unfortunately, people in Parliament didn't think she would make an ideal queen.

She's had two husbands before. We know this will upset your subjects.

But I'm not asking them to marry her!

Would Edward do the job he was born to do or marry the woman he loved? To his subjects' amazement and dismay, he chose Mrs Simpson — then simply gave up his throne.

In different ways Richard I, Henry VI, Victoria and Edward VIII 'weren't there' for their subjects. This made many people think of them as dead-loss rulers. Yet not many of their subjects wanted to get rid of them altogether. With the next two monarchs it was a different story ...

Chapter 5
A Job to Die For?

"I didn't sign up for this!"

Being seen as a dead loss was not the worst thing that could happen to a monarch. You could be driven out of your kingdom. You could be put in prison. And even worse, you could lose your head!

In the 1560s, while Elizabeth I ruled England, her beautiful cousin Mary, Queen of Scots, ruled the separate kingdom of Scotland. She wasn't a hard-working or very talented ruler, and she kept falling out with her top subjects. In 1567, they put her in prison – and made her pass the crown to her son.

"Your son will now rule in your place."

"But he's only one year old!"

"He'll still be better than you."

24

Two Queens in One Country

Mary escaped from prison and fled to England. There she started **plotting** to become Queen of England instead. Elizabeth wasn't having that. She had her cousin locked up – for 20 years! Even under lock and key Mary kept plotting. By 1587, Elizabeth had had enough. Mary was sentenced to death by having her head chopped off.

> This should never happen to a monarch. Let's hope it's a one-off.

Mary never got to rule England, but her grandson, Charles I, did. Amazingly, he also lost his head.

Imagine what Charles I and Mary, Queen of Scots, would have said if they'd ever met ...

Hello, Granny Mary, you won't know me: I'm Charles I, ex-King of England.

My goodness, whatever happened to you?

Oh, I had an argument with Parliament. They said they couldn't trust me to rule any more.

So they cut off your head?

Only after a major war. From 1642 to 1649. The English Civil War, they called it – although the Scots, Welsh and Irish got involved too.

So who became the next monarch?

No one. Parliament tried not having kings or queens for a bit.

"A kingdom without a king – I bet that didn't work."

"No, it didn't. One Member of Parliament, Oliver Cromwell, got too big for his boots and ruled just like a king himself."

"The nerve! He wasn't born for the job! Is he still ruling?"

"No, no, he died. Then in 1660, Parliament invited a proper king back to rule alongside them. My son, as it happens. Your great-grandson, Charles II."

"You can't beat a good monarch."

"No, but you can **behead** one you don't like!"

So there you have it. Ruling *could* be fun but now you know it wasn't always easy. What could have helped kings and queens in the past do a better job? Let's find out …

Top Tips
How NOT to be a Dead-loss Ruler

- Be old enough
- Preferably be male
- If you are female, be careful who you marry
- Try not to upset too many of your subjects, especially (in more modern times) Parliament
- Work hard, keep your mind on the job (and keep your head)
- Rule as long as you possibly can and, in order to achieve all this, wish yourself the best of luck!

But who says whether you're a dead cool ruler or a dead loss?

Although monarchs have great power, they don't always have the last word ...

All a Matter of Opinion

Today we remember some monarchs by nicknames. Elizabeth I is called 'Good Queen Bess' (dead cool). Mary I is known as 'Bloody Mary' (dead loss). But royal nicknames were often made up long after the monarchs died. While they were still alive, people may have seen them very differently.

> I shall be known as 'Brad the Brilliant'.

> That's what you think. *We'll* give you a nickname!

After reading all of that, would you still want to be a monarch? What sort of king or queen might you have been? A dead good ruler or a stone-cold dead loss? One thing's for sure – a lot can go wrong!

Timeline

Here are the kings and queens featured in this book with the dates they reigned. They were also often monarchs of more than one country.

Richard I
1189-1199
England

Edward V
1483
England and Wales

Henry VIII
1509-1547
England and Wales

Henry VI
1422-1461
England and Wales

Richard III
1483-1485
England and Wales

Edward VI
1547-1553
England and Wales

Mary I
1553-1558

England and Wales

Elizabeth I
1558-1603

England and Wales

Victoria
1837-1901

England, Wales, Scotland and Northern Ireland

Mary, Queen of Scots
1542-1567

Scotland

Charles I
1625-1649

England, Wales and Scotland

Edward VIII
1936

England, Wales, Scotland and Northern Ireland

Glossary

authority: power to give orders and make others obey you

behead: cut someone's head off

Civil War: war within a country between different groups of people

courtier: person who is part of a king or queen's court (where the king and queen live and work)

devote: give all your time to something

govern: rule or lead

invaders: group of people who attack a particular place as an enemy

Member of Parliament: person who helps run a country

monarch: ruler such as a king or queen

Parliament: group of people who make the laws for a country

plotting: planning in secret to do something bad

Prime Minister: chief Member of Parliament and head of a government

subjects: people who are ruled by a monarch

taxes: money paid to the government of a country by the people who live there

Index

authority 9, 15
Charles I 25–27, 31
child rulers 9–14, 24
courtiers 14, 21
Edward V 9–12, 30
Edward VI 13–14, 30
Edward VIII 23, 31
Elizabeth I 17–18, 24, 25, 29, 31
Henry VI 20–21, 30
Henry VIII 7, 30
invaders 5, 11, 12
Mary I 16–17, 29, 31
Mary, Queen of Scots 24–27, 31
monarchs 4–8, 17, 19, 21, 24, 28
nicknames 29
Oliver Cromwell 27
paintings 7, 13
Parliament 4, 21, 22, 23, 26–27, 28
Prime Ministers 4
Princes in the Tower 9–12
Richard I (the Lionheart) 19–20, 30
Richard III 9–10, 11–12, 30
royal duties 5, 6
Victoria 21-22, 31